The Half-Finished Heaven

Other Books by Tomas Tranströmer

17 Poems (1954)

Secrets on the Road (1958)

The Half-Finished Heaven (1962)

Resonance and Footprints (1966)

Night Vision (1970)

Pathways (1973)

Baltics (1974)

Truth Barriers (1978)

The Wild Market Square (1983)

For the Living and the Dead (1989)

Memories See Me (a prose memoir, 1993)

Grief Gondola (1996)

The
Half-Finished
Heaven

The Best Poems of Tomas Tranströmer

Chosen and Translated by

Robert Bly

Graywolf Press

Publication of this volume is made possible in part by a grant provided by the Minnesota State Arts Board through an appropriation by the Minnesota State Legislature, and by a grant from the National Endowment for the Arts. Significant support has also been provided by the Bush Foundation; Dayton's Project Imagine with support from Target Foundation; the McKnight Foundation; a grant made on behalf of the Stargazer Foundation; and other generous contributions from foundations, corporations, and individuals. To these organizations and individuals we offer our heartfelt thanks.

Funding for this title has been provided by the Swedish Council of America.

Some of these translations, a few in earlier versions, appeared in: *Twenty Poems of Tomas Tranströmer* (1970), *Night Vision* (1971), *Friends, You Drank Some Darkness: Three Swedish Poets, Ekelöf, Martinson, and Tranströmer* (1975), and *Truth Barriers* (1980). Some translations appeared as well in two compilations, *Selected Poems 1954–1986,* edited by Robert Hass (1987) and *For the Living and the Dead,* edited by Daniel Halpern (1996).

Particular thanks is due to Eva Bonnier, for many kindnesses.

Published by Graywolf Press
250 Third Avenue North, Suite 600
Minneapolis, MN 55401
All rights reserved.

www.graywolfpress.org

Published in the United States of America

ISBN: 978-1-55597-351-3

6 8 9 7 5

Library of Congress Control Number: 2001088643

Cover art: Vermeer, *Woman in Blue Reading a Letter.* From the collection of the Rijksmuseum, Amsterdam.

Cover design: Christa Schoenbrodt, Studio Haus

Contents

3   FROM
Pathways (1973)
Truth Barriers (1978)

4 FROM

The Wild Market Square (1983)
For the Living and the Dead (1989)
Grief Gondola (1996)

Upward into the Depths

1.

Tomas Tranströmer has a strange genius for the image; images rise seemingly without effort on his part. The wide space we feel in his poems perhaps occurs because the four or five main images in each poem come from widely separated sources in the psyche. His poems are a sort of railway station where trains that have come enormous distances stand briefly in the same building. One train may have some Russian snow on the undercarriage, and another may have Mediterranean flowers fresh in the compartments, and Ruhr soot on the roofs.

The poems are mysterious because the images have traveled a long way to get there. Mallarmé believed there should be mystery in poetry, and urged poets to get it, if necessary, by removing the links that tie the poem to its occasion in the real world. In Tranströmer's poems, the link to the worldly occasion is stubbornly kept, and yet the mystery and surprise never fade, even on many readings.

2.

There is a layer in our consciousness or memory, it seems, that runs alongside our life experience, but is not drawn from our life. It is perhaps older. "With his work, as with a glove, a man feels the universe," Tranströmer says. "Schubertiana" begins:

> Outside New York, dusk coming, a high place where with one
> glance you take in the houses where eight million human
> beings live.

The enormous city at night, he says, looks like "a spiral galaxy seen from the side." And he evokes scenes of coffee cups being pushed across desks, air-moved doors, fire escapes, people slumped over in the subway. Then he says:

> I know also—statistics to the side—that at this moment in
> some room down there Schubert is being played, and for
> that person the notes are more real than all the rest.

Tranströmer often edges toward ways of containing in words the before-birth intensities, the intensities not entirely *ours*. After all, what are notes? Sounds shaped by, say, a string quartet, contain almost no life stuff. They are pure sound vibrations, yet connected apparently to feelings that resonate somewhere inside us. Tomas Tranströmer ends a prose poem, "At Funchal," saying,

> The innermost paradox, the underground garage flowers,
> the vent toward the good dark. A drink that bubbles in an
> empty glass. An amplifier that magnifies silence. A path that
> grows over after every step. A book that can only be read in
> the dark.

Some works of art do cross the line that separates worlds. A poem of that sort might include an amplifier and silence, an underground garage and flowers, the banal outer world and a mysterious underworld. In this double world it is difficult to keep one's balance, and it's best to leave all rhetoric out.

> It's been a hard winter, but summer is here and the fields
> want us to walk upright. Every man unimpeded, but careful, as
> when you stand up in a small boat. I remember a day in Africa:
> on the banks of the Chari, there were many boats, an atmosphere positively friendly, the men almost blue-black in color
> with three parallel scars on each cheek (meaning the Sara

tribe). I am welcomed on a boat—it's a canoe hollowed from a dark tree. The canoe is incredibly wobbly, even when you sit on your heels. A balancing act. If you have the heart on the left side you have to lean a bit to the right, nothing in the pockets, no big arm movements, please, all rhetoric has to be left behind. Precisely: rhetoric is impossible here. The canoe glides out over the water.

(from "Standing Up")

It was Rilke who created the metaphor that poets are "bees of the invisible." Making honey of the invisible suggests that the artist remains close to his own earthly history, but moves as well toward the spiritual and the invisible. As an artist, Tranströmer seems to be steadied by such efforts, and by the example of other European poets who have done so.

Tomas's love of Schubert carries him to the boundary between worlds; and at such a boundary, he sees landscapes ordinarily hidden:

The five instruments play. I go home through warm woods
   where the earth is springy under my feet,
curl up like someone still unborn, sleep, roll on so weightlessly into the future, suddenly understand that plants
   are thinking.

Art helps us, he says, as a banister helps the climber on a dark stairwell. The banister finds its own way in the dark. In Schubert, "happiness and suffering weigh exactly the same." The depths are above us and below us at the same instant. The melody line is a

   stubborn humming sound that this instant is with us
   upward into
   the depths.

Tranströmer suspects that as an artist he is merely a way for the "Memory" to get out into the world. Even at seventeen he was aware that the dead "wanted to have their portraits painted." He says we are "lowered" into the past. In "About History," he says we are like a microphone that has been lowered under the ice of a spring lake.

His poem, "December Evening, '72," begins:

Here I come the invisible man, perhaps in the employ
of some huge Memory that wants to live at this moment.
    And I drive by

the white church that's locked up. A saint made of wood is
    inside,
smiling helplessly, as if someone had taken his glasses.

Tranströmer is an elegant and humorous servant of the "Memory." In "Guard Duty" he says:

Task: to be where I am.
Even when I'm in this solemn and absurd
role: I am still the place
where creation works on itself.

Dawn comes, the sparse tree trunks
take on color now, the frostbitten
forest flowers form a silent search party
after something that has disappeared in the dark.

But to be where I am . . . and to wait.
I am full of anxiety, obstinate, confused.
Things not yet happened are already here!
I feel that. They're just out there:

a murmuring mass outside the barrier.
They can only slip in one by one.
They want to slip in. Why? They do
one by one. I am the turnstile.

Even after hard work during the day, he has high spirits:

Allegro

After a black day, I play Haydn,
and feel a little warmth in my hands.

The keys are ready. Kind hammers fall.
The sound is spirited, green, and full of silence.

The sounds says that freedom exists
and someone pays no taxes to Caesar.

I shove my hands in my haydnpockets
and act like a man who is calm about it all.

I raise my haydnflag. The signal is:
"We do not surrender. But want peace."

The music is a house of glass standing on a slope;
rocks are flying, rocks are rolling.

The rocks roll straight through the house
but every pane of glass is still whole.

3.

Tomas Tranströmer was an only child, born in Stockholm in
1931, on April 15. His father and mother divorced when he was
three; he and his mother lived after that in an apartment in the

working-class district of Stockholm. As a student, he pursued music and psychology.

The early fifties were a rather formal time, both here and in Sweden, and Tranströmer began by writing highly formal poems, some in iambic and Alcaic meter. His first book, *17 Poems*, published in 1954, which glowed with several baroque elements, contained only seventeen poems, but people noticed the power of it immediately. Tranströmer decided to make his living as a psychologist. For some years he worked at a boys' prison in Linköping. The boys he counseled in that prison evidently took in a lively impression of him. Someone sent me a clipping from Sweden during that time, which recounted the adventures of a youth who had escaped a short time before from the Linköping reformatory. It transpired that he registered in various Swedish hotels and motels as "T. Tranströmer, psychologist."

In 1965 he moved with his wife Monica and his two daughters, Paula and Emma, to Västerås, a town about forty miles west of Stockholm. He continued to work as a psychologist, this time for a labor organization funded by the State. He helped juvenile delinquents reenter society, persons with physical disabilities choose a career, and he counseled parole offenders and those in drug rehabilitation. Once, during a reading in New York, a member of the audience asked him if his work had affected his poetry. He did reply, but mentioned how odd it seemed that so few people asked him: "How has your poetry affected your work?" In a printed interview later, he remarked that he had early learned to admire active syntax when composing a poem. When counseling juveniles, he urged them to do likewise. If they were liable to say, "I found myself in this apartment . . ." or "As it happened, I . . . ," he urged them to say, "I broke the window and crawled in."

His wife Monica, who was trained as a nurse, has accepted various jobs during their marriage, sometimes with newborn children and their mothers; for a time she was in charge of

Vietnamese refugees who were resettling in Sweden. When one sees Monica and Tomas together, one can still glimpse in the room the freshness of their first meetings.

Tranströmer's poems have been translated into many languages, something like thirty-eight so far. During the seventies and eighties, a number of American poets translated his work, including May Swenson, Samuel Charters, Joanna Bankier, Eric Sellin, and in Great Britain we might mention Robin Fulton and John F. Deane. Robert Hass edited a selected poems for Ecco Press in 1987.

In Europe the praise for his poems has steadily grown. He has received almost every important poetry prize in Europe, including the Petrarch Prize in Germany, the Bonnier Award for Poetry, the Pilot Prize in 1988, the Nordic Council Prize in 1990, the Swedish Academy's Nordic Prize in 1991, and the Horst Bieneck Prize in 1992.

4.

Tomas Tranströmer's poems are a luminous example of the ability of good poetry in one culture to travel to another culture and arrive. As Tranströmer said in a letter to the Hungarian poets, published in the magazine Uj Iras in 1977, "Poetry has an advantage from the start. . . . Poetry requires no heavy, vulnerable apparatus that has to be lugged around. . . ."

Tomas writes playfully about technology. He has remarked that when he first began to write, in the early fifties, it still seemed possible to write a nature poem into which nothing technological entered. Now, he says, many objects created by technology have become almost parts of nature; and the fact that Sweden has a highly developed technology is always visible in his recent poems. He doesn't exile technology, nor does technology dominate the poem:

> and every year the factory buildings go down another
> eighth of an inch—the earth is gulping them slowly.

Paws no one can identify leave a print
on the glossiest artifacts dreamed up here.

. . . .

And no one knows what will happen, we only know
the chain breaks and grows back together all the time.

(from "Traffic")

Even in the countryside of Sweden there are hints:

All at once I notice the hills on the other side of the lake:
their pine has been clear-cut. They resemble the shaved skull-
sections of a patient about to have a brain operation.

(from "For Mats and Laila")

Swedish society is most famously a welfare society, *the* wel-
fare society; it is perhaps the first society in history that has had
the will and the wealth to insist on the abolition of poverty.
But it is also a technological society like ours, and one given
to secular solutions. Tranströmer reports how difficult it is in
Sweden to keep in touch with certain kinds of tenderness. In
"Below Freezing," he writes:

We are at a party that doesn't love us. Finally the party lets the
mask fall and shows what it is: a shunting station for freight
cars. In the fog cold giants stand on their tracks. A scribble of
chalk on the car doors.

One can't say it aloud, but there is a lot of repressed vio-
lence here. That is why the furnishings seem so heavy. And
why it is so difficult to see the other thing present: a spot of
sun that moves over the house walls and slips over the un-
aware forest of flickering faces, a biblical saying never set
down: "Come unto me, for I am as full of contradictions as
you."

He returns again and again to a childhood home in Runmarö, an island in the archipelago off the east coast of Sweden; and he is as deeply attached to it as Jean Giono to the Vaucluse, or Hardy to "Wessex." The long poem "Baltics," which Samuel Charters translated, draws its images from the landscape and history of that island, out of which his grandfather worked as a ship pilot. On his father's side, he comes from pilots who guided ships among the islands in the Stockholm Archipelago.

5.

In his work, Tranströmer is always aware of something approaching over the border. The title of his fourth book, *Sanningsbarriären,* literally "The Truth Barrier," suggests a customs house, or the customs table at an airport. *Sanningsbarriären* also contains a slight pun on the English phrase, "sound barrier."

As "Start of a Late Autumn Novel" begins, he is lying half asleep on the island, and hears a thumping sound outside. It seems to vanish and return. Or perhaps there is some being inside the wall who is knocking:

> someone who belongs to the other world, but got left here
> anyway, he thumps, wants to go back. Too late. Wasn't on
> time down here, wasn't on time up there, didn't make it on
> board in time.

Dreams surely come from over the border. "Citoyens" rose from a dream Tranströmer had the night following an automobile accident (the one he describes in "Solitude"). Danton with his pockmarked face appeared, but the dreamer could only see half his face, as we only see one side of the moon. Danton seemed to be standing on stilts:

I saw his face from underneath:
like the pitted moon, half lit, half in mourning.
I wanted to say something.
A weight in the chest: the lead weight
that makes the clocks go,
makes the hands go around: Year I, Year II . . .
A pungent odor as from sawdust in tiger cages.
And—as always in dreams—no sun.
But the alley walls
shone as they curved away
down toward the waiting-room, the curved space,
the waiting room where we all . . .

The alley walls curve away toward a "waiting room," which reminded Tranströmer of the hospital lobby where he waited so often to see his mother while she was dying of cancer. "The waiting room where we all . . ."

During the eighties Tranströmer wrote a masterpiece centered on the Dutch painter Vermeer and his painting *Woman in Blue Reading a Letter.* The poem evokes the terror lying behind that calm canvas.

It's not a sheltered world. The noise begins over there, on the
    other side of the wall
where the alehouse is
with its laughter and quarrels, its rows of teeth, its tears,
    its chiming of clocks,
and the psychotic brother-in-law, the murderer, in whose
    presence everyone feels fear.
. . . .

She is eight months pregnant, two hearts beating inside her.
The wall behind her holds a crinkly map of Terra Incognita.

We see a chair covered with a blue fabric:

Just breathe. An unidentifiable blue fabric has been tacked to
    the chairs.
Gold-headed tacks flew in with astronomical speed
and stopped smack there
as if they had always been stillness and nothing else.

The ears experience a buzz, perhaps it's depth or perhaps height.
It's the pressure from the other side of the wall,
. . . .

And what is empty turns its face to us
and whispers:
"I am not empty, I am open."

A second masterpiece, from the nineties, is "Grief Gondola #2"
(the title is from a piano piece by Franz Liszt). We feel again
Tranströmer's devotion to music. Richard Wagner was married
to Cosima, the daughter of Franz Liszt, and the two of them
were living in Venice in 1882. The father-in-law, Liszt, came to
visit them. There was something heavy in the visit, and Wagner
in fact died soon after. In the opening lines, Tranströmer play-
fully calls Wagner King Midas:

                              . . . King Midas—
    I mean the one who turns everyone he touches into Wagner.

He goes on:

    Wagner has received the Mark . . .
    . . . .

    The heavily loaded gondola carries their lives, two return
        tickets and a one-way.

Tranströmer finds an amazing way to allow those moments in
Venice to reach forward into the European future:

Liszt has composed a few chords so heavy one should send
    them
off to the Institute for Mineralogical Studies in Padua.
Meteorites!
Far too heavy to stay where they are, they start sinking and
    sinking down through the coming years until they reach
the year of the Brownshirts.

Tranströmer doesn't leave out his own life; he talks of himself:

I dreamt that I had sketched piano keys out
on the kitchen table. I played on them, without a sound.
Neighbors came by to listen.

Back to Liszt:

When Liszt plays tonight he holds down the sea-pedal so that
    the ocean's green force
rises through the floor and penetrates every stone of the building.
Good evening to you, beautiful deep!

6.

Tranströmer's life was interrupted tragically in 1990, when he suffered a stroke. His blood pressure had always been high; he had been traveling a lot and was tired. He survived the stroke, but the right side of his body has remained partially paralyzed. The stroke impaired his ability to find and speak words as well. Nevertheless his spirits remain high; he continues to compose poems, and has recently completed a group of new haikus.

In 2001, Tomas and Monica moved from Västerås to an apartment in Stockholm, near the old neighborhood where Tomas once lived as a boy. The town of Västerås gave an elaborate farewell ceremony for Monica and Tomas, complete with medieval music and a choir and formal readings of his poems at the old castle. He brought his piano along, and in the Stockholm apartment, he plays that piano brilliantly with his left hand. Composers in Sweden have begun to send him piano works that they have newly written for his left hand. That detail suggests how much affection there is in Sweden for Tomas and his poetry.

Romanesque Arches

Tourists have crowded into the half-dark of the enormous
    Romanesque church.
Vault opening behind vault and no perspective.
A few candle flames flickered.
An angel whose face I couldn't see embraced me
and his whisper went all through my body:
"Don't be ashamed to be a human being, be proud!
Inside you one vault after another opens endlessly.
You'll never be complete, and that's as it should be."
Tears blinded me
as we were herded out into the fiercely sunlit piazza,
together with Mr. and Mrs. Jones, Herr Tanaka and Signora
    Sabatini;
within each of them vault after vault opened endlessly.

So here we are. We have a funny, brave, affectionate poet of great depth. He fought for his way—essentially a religious way—against enormous opposition during the sixties and seventies from the doctrinaire critics and Maoist skinflints who dominated Swedish intellectual life at that time. He didn't waver. In "Fire Script" he says to his wife,

> The night heavens gave off moos.
> We stole milk from the cosmos and survived.

—Robert Bly

1

POEMS FROM:

17 Poems (1954)
Secrets on the Road (1958)
The Half-Finished Heaven (1962)

Evening—Morning

The moon-mast has rotted, and the sail crinkled.
A seagull sails drunkenly over the sea.
The thick cube of dock looks charred. Bushes crouch down in
    the dark.

On the doorstep. The sunrise pushes again and again
through the gray stone-gates of the ocean, and the sun sparkles
near the earth. Half-suffocated summer gods grope in the sea
    mist.

Storm

The man on a walk suddenly meets the old
giant oak like an elk turned to stone with
its enormous antlers against the dark green castle wall
          of the fall ocean.

Storm from the north. It's nearly time for the
rowanberries to ripen. Awake in the night he
hears the constellations far above the oak
          stamping in their stalls.

The Man Awakened by a Song above His Roof

Morning, May rain. The city is silent still
as a sheepherder's hut. Streets silent. And in
the sky a plane motor is rumbling bluish green.—
    The window is open.

The dream of the man stretched out sleeping
becomes at that instant transparent. He turns, begins
to grope for the tool of his consciousness—
    almost in space.

Track

2 A.M.: moonlight. The train has stopped
out in a field. Far-off sparks of light from a town,
flickering coldly on the horizon.

As when a man goes so deep into his dream
he will never remember that he was there
when he returns again to his room.

Or when a person goes so deep into a sickness
that his days all become some flickering sparks, a swarm,
feeble and cold on the horizon.

The train is entirely motionless.
2 o'clock: strong moonlight, few stars.

Kyrie

At times my life suddenly opens its eyes in the dark.
A feeling of masses of people pushing blindly
through the streets, excitedly, toward some miracle,
while I remain here and no one sees me.

It is like the child who falls asleep in terror
listening to the heavy thumps of his heart.
For a long, long time till morning puts his light in the locks
and the doors of darkness open.

After the Attack

The sick boy.
Locked in a vision
with tongue stiff as a horn.

He sits with his back toward the painting of a wheatfield.
The bandage around his jaw reminds one of an embalming.
His spectacles are thick as a diver's. Nothing has any answer
and is sudden as a telephone ringing in the night.

But the painting there. It is a landscape that makes one feel
  peaceful even though the wheat is a golden storm.
Blue, fiery blue sky and driving clouds. Beneath in the yellow
  waves
some white shirts are sailing: threshers—they cast no shadow.

At the far end of the field a man seems to be looking this way.
  A broad hat leaves his face in shadow.
He seems to look at the dark shape in the room here, as
  though to help.
Gradually the painting begins to stretch and open behind the
  boy who is sick
and sunk in himself. It throws sparks and makes noise. Every
  wheathead throws off light as if to wake him up!
The other man—in the wheat—makes a sign.

He has come nearer.
No one notices it.

Balakirev's Dream (1905)

The black grand piano, the gleamy spider,
stood quivering in the center of its music net.

The sounds in the concert room composed a land
where stones were no heavier than dew.

Balakirev though fell asleep during the music
and in his dream he saw the Czar's carriage.

It was rolling over the cobblestones
and straight on into the croaking, cawing night.

He was sitting alone inside the cab watching,
also he was running alongside on the road.

He knew the trip had been long already,
and the face on his watch showed years, not hours.

A field appears in which a plough stood,
and the plough was a bird just leaving the ground.

A bay appeared where a destroyer stood,
ice-locked, lights out, people on deck.

The carriage rolled away over the ice, the wheels
spinning and spinning with a sound like silk.

A destroyer of the second class: *Sevastapol.*
He was on it. The crew came toward him.

"If you can play, you won't have to die."
Then they showed him an amazing instrument.

It looked like a tuba, or an old phonograph,
or a section of some unheard-of machine.

Helpless and afraid, suddenly he realized: it is
the device that is used to power naval ships.

He turned to the sailor standing nearest,
waved his hand in despair, and said:

"Imitate me, make the sign of the cross, make the sign!"
The sailor stared full of grief like a blind man,

opened his arms out, let his head fall—
he hung there as if nailed to the air.

Here are the drums. Here are the drums. Applause!
Balakirev woke up from his dream.

Applause-wings were flapping about the room.
He watched the man at the grand piano stand up.

Outdoors a strike had darkened the city streets.
Carriages for hire rolled swiftly through the night.

Milij Balakirev (1837–1910)
Russian composer

The Couple

They turn the light off, and its white globe glows
an instant and then dissolves, like a tablet
in a glass of darkness. Then a rising.
The hotel walls shoot up into heaven's darkness.

Their movements have grown softer, and they sleep,
but their most secret thoughts begin to meet
like two colors that meet and run together
on the wet paper in a schoolboy's painting.

It is dark and silent. The city however has come nearer
tonight. With its windows turned off. Houses have come.
They stand packed and waiting very near,
a mob of people with blank faces.

Allegro

After a black day, I play Haydn,
and feel a little warmth in my hands.

The keys are ready. Kind hammers fall.
The sound is spirited, green, and full of silence.

The sound says that freedom exists
and someone pays no taxes to Caesar.

I shove my hands in my haydnpockets
and act like a man who is calm about it all.

I raise my haydnflag. The signal is:
"We do not surrender. But want peace."

The music is a house of glass standing on a slope;
rocks are flying, rocks are rolling.

The rocks roll straight through the house
but every pane of glass is still whole.

Lamento

He put the pen down.
It lies there without moving.
It lies there without moving in empty space.
He put the pen down.

So much that can neither be written nor kept inside!
His body is stiffened by something happening far away
though the curious overnight bag beats like a heart.

Outside, the late spring.
From the foliage a whistling—people or birds?
And the cherry trees in bloom pat the heavy trucks on the way
    home.

Weeks go by.
Slowly night comes.
Moths settle down on the pane:
small pale telegrams from the world.

The Tree and the Sky

The tree is walking around in the rain
moving past us in the squishy gray.
It has a job to do. It picks life out of the rain
like a blackbird in a cherry orchard.

As soon as the rain stops, the tree stops too.
It simply stands, motionless in the clear nights,
waiting just as we do for that moment
when snowflakes will throw themselves out in space.

A Winter Night

The storm puts its lips to the house
    and blows to make a sound.
I sleep restlessly, turn over, with closed
    eyes read the book of the storm.

But the child's eyes grow huge in the dark
    and the storm whimpers for the child.
Both love to see the swinging lamp.
    Both are halfway toward speech.

Storms have childlike hands and wings.
    The caravan bolts off toward Lapland
and the house senses the constellation of nails
    holding its walls together.

The night is quiet above our floor
    (where all the died-away footsteps
are lying like sunken leaves in a pond)
    but outside the night is wild!

A more serious storm is moving over us all.
    It puts its lips to our soul
and blows to make a sound. We're afraid
    the storm will blow everything inside us away.

Dark Shape Swimming

A Stone Age painting
on a Sahara boulder:
a shadowy shape that swims
on some ancient fresh river.

With no weapon, and no plan,
neither at rest nor hurrying,
the swimmer is parted from his shadow
which is slipping along the bottom.

He has fought to get free
from millions of sleeping leaves,
to make it to the other shore
and join his shadow again.

The Half-Finished Heaven

Cowardice breaks off on its path.
Anguish breaks off on its path.
The vulture breaks off in its flight.

The eager light runs into the open,
even the ghosts take a drink.

And our paintings see the air,
red beasts of the ice-age studios.

Everything starts to look around.
We go out in the sun by hundreds.

Every person is a half-open door
leading to a room for everyone.

The endless field under us.

Water glitters between the trees.

The lake is a window into the earth.

Nocturne

I drive through a village at night, the houses step out
into the headlights—they are awake now, they want a drink.
Houses, barns, nameposts, deserted trailers—now
they take on life. Human beings sleep:

some can sleep peacefully, others have tense faces
as though in hard training for eternity.
They don't dare to let go even in deep sleep.
They wait like lowered gates while the mystery rolls past.

Outside town the road sweeps on a long time through the
    forest.
Trees, trees silent in a pact with each other.
They have a melodramatic color, as if in firelight.
How clear every leaf is! They follow me all the way home.

I lie about to fall asleep, I see unknown images
and signs sketching themselves behind the eyelids
on the wall of the dark. In the slot between waking and sleep
a large letter tries to get in without quite succeeding.

2

Open and Closed Space

With his work, as with a glove, a man feels the universe.
At noon he rests a while, and lays the gloves aside on a shelf.
There they suddenly start growing, grow huge
and make the whole house dark from inside.

The darkened house is out in the April winds.
"Amnesty," the grass whispers, "amnesty."
A boy runs along with an invisible string that goes right up into
    the sky.
There his wild dream of the future flies like a kite, bigger than
    his town.

Farther to the north, you see from a hill the blue matting of fir
    trees
on which the shadows of the clouds
do not move.
No, they are moving.

From an African Diary (1963)

In the painting of the kitsch Congolese artists
The figures are skinny as insects, their human energy
   saddened.
The road from one way of life to another is hard.
The one who has arrived has a long way to go.

A young African found a tourist lost among the huts.
He couldn't decide whether to make him a friend or object of
   blackmail.
The indecision upset him. They parted in confusion.

Europeans stick near their cars as if the cars were Mama.
Cicadas are strong as electric razors. The cars drive home.
Soon the lovely darkness comes and washes the dirty clothes.
   Sleep.
The one who has arrived has a long way to go.

Perhaps a migratory flock of handshakes would help.
Perhaps letting the truth escape from books would help.
We have to go farther.

The student studies all night, studies and studies so he can be
   free.
When the examination is over, he turns into a stair-rung for the
   next man.
A hard road.
The one who has arrived has a long way to go.

Morning Bird Songs

I wake up my car;
pollen covers the windshield.
I put my dark glasses on.
The bird songs all turn dark.

Meanwhile someone is buying a paper
at the railroad station
not far from a big freight car
reddened all over with rust.
It shimmers in the sun.

The whole universe is full.

A cool corridor cuts through the spring warmth;
a man comes hurrying past
describing how someone right up in the main office
has been telling lies about him.

Through a backdoor in the landscape
the magpie arrives,
black and white, bird of the death-goddess.
A blackbird flies back and forth
until the whole scene becomes a charcoal drawing,
except for the white clothes on the line:
a Palestrina choir.

The whole universe is full!

Fantastic to feel how my poem is growing
while I myself am shrinking.

It's getting bigger, it's taking my place,
it's pressing against me.
It has shoved me out of the nest.
The poem is finished.

Summer Grass

So much has happened.
Reality has eaten away so much of us.
But summer, at last.

A great airport—the control tower leads down
load after load with chilled
people from space.

Grass and flowers—we are landing.
The grass has a green foreman.
I go and check in.

About History

I.

One March day I walked down to the lake shore to listen.
The ice was blue as the sky. And breaking up in the sun.
The sun whispers into a microphone under the ice.
There's a seething and burbling. Far out it sounds like a sheet
    being snapped.
The whole thing is like History: our present. We are lowered
    into it, we listen.

II.

Conferences resemble unstable and flying islands.
Afterward: a long shaky bridge of compromise.
All the traffic passes over that bridge beneath stars,
beneath the pale faces of children not yet born
who are cast off, nameless as grains of rice.

III.

In 1926, Goethe visited Africa disguised as Gide and noticed
    it.
Some faces get clearer through what they've seen after death.
When the daily news from Algeria arrived on the radio,
I saw a big house and all the windows in the house were dark
except one. Dreyfus's face looked out from that one.

IV.

Radical and Reactionary live together as in a miserable
    marriage,
diminished by each other, leaning on each other.
But we, their children, have to find our own road.
Each problem cries out in a private language!
Walk down any path where there is a trace of truth.

V.

In a field not far from the subdivisions
a newspaper has been lying for months, full of news.
It is aging because of days and nights, rain and sun.
It's on its way to becoming a plant, a cabbage head. It's starting
    to join the field,
like an old memory gradually changing into you.

After a Death

Once there was a shock
that left behind a long, shimmering comet tail.
It keeps us inside. It makes the TV pictures snowy.
It settles in cold drops on the telephone wires.

One can still go slowly on skis in the winter sun
through brush where a few leaves hang on.
They resemble pages torn from old telephone directories.
Names swallowed by the cold.

It is still beautiful to hear the heart beat
but often the shadow seems more real than the body.
The samurai looks insignificant
beside his armor of black dragon scales.

Under Pressure

Powerful engines from the blue sky.
We live on a construction site where everything shivers,
where the ocean depths can suddenly open.
A hum in seashells and telephones.

You can see beauty if you look quickly to the side.
The heavy grainfields run together in one yellow river.
The restless shadows in my head want to go out there.
They want to crawl in the grain and turn into something gold.

Night finally. At midnight I go to bed.
The dinghy sets out from the ship.
On the water you are alone.
The dark hull of society keeps on going.

Slow Music

The building not open today. The sun crowds in through the
    windowpanes
and warms the upper side of the desk
which is strong enough to bear the fate of others.

Today we are outdoors, on the long wide slope.
Some have dark clothes. If you stand in the sun, and shut your
    eyes,
you feel as if you were being slowly blown forward.

I come too seldom down to the sea. But now I have come,
among good-sized stones with peaceful backs.
The stones have been gradually walking backwards out of the
    sea.

Out in the Open

I.

Late autumn labyrinth.
At the entry to the woods a thrown-away bottle.
Go in. Woods are silent abandoned houses this time of year.
Just a few sounds now: as if someone were moving twigs
    around carefully with pincers
or as if an iron hinge were whining feebly inside a thick trunk.
Frost has breathed on the mushrooms and they have shriveled
    up.
They look like objects and clothing left behind by people
    who've disappeared.
It will be dark soon. The thing to do now is to get out
and find the landmarks again: the rusty machine out in the
    field
and the house on the other side of the lake, a reddish square
    intense as a bouillon cube.

II.

A letter from America drove me out again, started me walking
through the luminous June night in the empty suburban streets
among newborn districts without memories, cool as
    blueprints.

Letter in my pocket. Half-mad, lost walking, it is a kind of
    prayer.
Over there evil and good actually have faces.
For the most part with us it's a fight between roots, numbers,
    shades of light.

The people who run death's errands for him don't shy from
    daylight.

They rule from glass offices. They mill about in the bright sun.
They lean forward over a desk, and throw a look to the side.

Far off I found myself standing in front of one of the new
    buildings.
Many windows flowed together there into a single window.
In it the luminous night sky was caught, and the walking trees.
It was a mirrorlike lake with no waves, turned on edge in the
    summer night.

Violence seemed unreal
for a few moments.

III.

Sun burning. The plane comes in low
throwing a shadow shaped like a giant cross that rushes over
    the ground.
A man is sitting in the field poking at something.
The shadow arrives.
For a fraction of a second he is right in the center of the cross.

I have seen the cross hanging in the cool church vaults.
At times it resembles a split-second snapshot of something
moving at tremendous speed.

Solitude

Right here I was nearly killed one night in February.
My car slewed on the ice, sideways,
into the other lane. The oncoming cars—
their headlights—came nearer.

My name, my daughters, my job
slipped free and fell behind silently,
farther and farther back. I was anonymous,
like a schoolboy in a lot surrounded by enemies.

The approaching traffic had powerful lights.
They shone on me while I turned and turned
the wheel in a transparent fear that moved like eggwhite.
The seconds lengthened out—making more room—
they grew long as hospital buildings.

It felt as if you could just take it easy
and loaf a bit
before the smash came.

Then firm land appeared: a helping sandgrain
or a marvelous gust of wind. The car took hold
and fishtailed back across the road.
A signpost shot up, snapped off—a ringing sound—
tossed into the dark.

Came all quiet. I sat there in my seatbelt
and watched someone tramp through the blowing snow
to see what had become of me.

II.

I have been walking a while
on the frozen Swedish fields
and I have seen no one.

In other parts of the world
people are born, live, and die
in a constant human crush.

To be visible all the time—to live
in a swarm of eyes—
surely that leaves its mark on the face.
Features overlaid with clay.

The low voices rise and fall
as they divide up
heaven, shadows, grains of sand.

I have to be by myself
ten minutes every morning,
ten minutes every night,
—and nothing to be done!

We all line up to ask each other for help.

Millions.

One.

Breathing Space July

The man who lies on his back under huge trees
is also up in them. He branches out into thousands of tiny
    branches.
He sways back and forth,
he sits in a catapult chair that hurtles forward in slow motion.

The man who stands down at the dock screws up his eyes
    against the water.
Docks get old faster than men.
They have silver-gray posts and boulders in their gut.
The dazzling light drives straight in.

The man who spends the whole day in an open boat
moving over the luminous bays
will fall asleep at last inside the shade of his blue lamp
as the islands crawl like huge moths over the globe.

The Open Window

I shaved one morning standing
by the open window
on the second story.
Switched on the razor.
It started to hum.
A heavier and heavier whirr.
Grew to a roar.
Grew to a helicopter.
And a voice—the pilot's—pierced
the noise, shouting:
"Keep your eyes open!
You're seeing this for the last time!"
Rose.
Floated low over the summer.
The small things I love, have they any weight?
So many dialects of green.
And especially the red of housewalls.
Beetles glittered in the dung, in the sun.
Cellars pulled up by the roots
sailed through the air.
Industry.
Printing presses crawled along.
People at that instant
were the only things motionless.
They observe their moments of silence.
And the dead in the churchyard especially
held still
like those who posed in the infancy of the camera.

Fly low!
I didn't know which way
to turn my head—
my sight was divided
like a horse's.

Preludes

I.

I shy from something that comes scraping crossways through
   the blizzard.
Fragment out of what is to come.
A wall gotten loose. Something eyeless. Hard.
A face of teeth!
A wall, alone. Or is a house there,
even though I can't see it?
The future . . . an army of empty houses
feeling their way forward in the falling snow.

II.

Two truths approach each other. One comes from inside, the
   other from outside,
and where they meet we have a chance to catch sight of
   ourselves.

The man who sees what's about to take place cries out wildly:
   "Stop!
Anything, if only I don't have to know myself."

And a boat exists that wants to tie up on shore—it's trying right
   here—
in fact it will try thousands of times yet.

Out of the darkness of the woods a long boathook appears,
   pokes in through the open window,
in among the guests who are getting warm dancing.

III.

The apartment where I lived over half of my life has to be cleaned out. It's already empty of everything. The anchor has let go—despite the continuing weight of grief it is the lightest apartment in the whole city. Truth doesn't need any furniture. My life has just completed a big circle and come back to its starting place: a room blown out. Things I've lived through here become visible on the walls like Egyptian paintings, murals from the inside of the grave chamber. But the scenes are growing fainter, because the light is getting too strong. The windows have got larger. The empty apartment is a large telescope held up to the sky. It is silent as a Quaker service. All you can hear are the doves in the backyard, their cooing.

The Bookcase

It was moved out of the apartment after her death. It stood empty several days, before I put the books in, all the cloth-bound ones, the heavy ones. Somehow during it all I had also let some grave earth slip in. Something came from underneath, rose gradually and implacably like an enormous mercury column. A man was not to turn his head away.

The dark volumes, faces closed. They resembled the faces of those Algerians I saw at the zone border at Friedrichstrasse waiting for the East German People's Police to stamp their identity books. My own passbook lay for a long time in the glass cubicles. And the dusky air I saw that day in Berlin I see again in the bookcase. There is some ancient despair in there, that tastes of Passchendaele and the Versailles Peace Treaty, maybe even older than that. Those massive black tomes—I come back to them—they are in their way passports themselves, and they have got so thick because people have had to collect so many official stamps on them over centuries. Obviously a man can't overestimate the amount of baggage he's expected to have, now that it's starting to go, now that you finally . . .

All the old historians are there, they get their chance to stand up and see into our family life. You can't hear a thing, but the lips are moving all the time behind the pane ("Passchendaele" . . .). It reminds me of that tale of an ancient office building (this is a pure ghost story), a building where portraits of long dead gentlemen hung on the wall behind glass, and one morning the office workers found some mist on the inside of the glass. The dead had begun to breathe during the night.

The bookcase is even stronger. Looks straight from zone one to the next! A glimmery skin, the glimmery skin on a dark river that the room has to see its own face in. And turning the head is not allowed.

Outskirts

Men in overalls the same color as earth rise from a ditch.
It's a transitional place, in stalemate, neither country nor city.
Construction cranes on the horizon want to take the big leap,
    but the clocks are against it.
Concrete piping scattered around laps at the light with cold
    tongues.
Auto-body shops occupy old barns.
Stones throw shadows as sharp as objects on the moon
    surface.
And these sites keep on getting bigger
like the land bought with Judas' silver: "a potter's field for
    burying strangers."

Going with the Current

Talking and talking with friends I saw heard behind their faces
the current
dragging with it those who want to go and those who don't.

And I saw a creature with its eyes glued together
who wants to leap right into the middle of the stream
throw itself out without a shiver
in a ravenous thirst for the simple answer.

Faster and faster the water pulls

as when a river narrows down and shoots over
into rapids—I stopped to rest at a spot like that
after a drive through dry woods

one evening in June: the transistor told me the latest
on the Extra Session: Kosygin, Eban.
One or two thoughts bored their way in despairingly.
One or two men drown in the village.

And huge masses of water plough by under the suspension
bridge. Down comes the timber! Some trunks
just shoot straight ahead like torpedoes. Others turn
crossways, sluggish, and spin helplessly away,

and others follow their nose onto the riverbank,
steer in among stones and rubbish, get wedged,
then in a pile turn up toward the sky like folded hands,

prayers drowned in the roar . . .

I saw heard it from a suspension bridge
in a cloud of gnats
together with a few boys. Their bicycles
buried in the bushes—only the horns
stood up.

Traffic

The semitrailer crawls through the fog.
It is the lengthened shadow of a dragonfly larva
crawling over the murky lakebottom.

Headlights cross among dripping branches.
You can't see the other driver's face.
Light overflows through the pines.

We have come, shadows chassis from all directions
in failing light, we go in tandem after each other,
past each other sweep on in a modest roar

into the open where the industries are brooding,
and every year the factory buildings go down another
eighth of an inch—the earth is gulping them slowly.

Paws no one can identify leave a print
on the glossiest artifacts dreamed up here.
Pollen is determined to live in asphalt.

But the horse-chestnut trees loom up first, melancholy
as if they intended to produce clusters of iron gloves
rather than white flowers, and past them

the reception room—a fluorescent light out of order
blinks off and on. Some magic door is around here! Open!
and look downward, through the reversed periscope,

down to the great mouths, the huge buried pipes
where algae is growing like the beards on dead men
and the Cleaner swims on in his overcoat of slime

and his strokes weaker and weaker, he will be choked soon.
And no one knows what will happen, we only know
the chain breaks and grows back together all the time.

Night Duty

I.

During the night I am down there with the ballast
I am one of those dead weights that say nothing,
that keep the sloop from turning over!
Fuzzy-edged faces in the dark, like stones.
All they can do is hiss: "Don't touch me."

II.

And other voices push through, the listener
is slipping over the luminous radio
dial like a slender shadow.
The language marches in perfect step with boots.
Therefore: go out and pick a new language!

III.

The wolf is here! Our helper and friend!
And against the windows he lays his tongue.
The valley is full of crawling ax-handles.
The night jet roars over the sky
as if it were a wheelchair running on its rims.

IV.

They are digging the place up. But it's quiet now.
In the empty cemetery under the elms:
an empty steam shovel. Its bucket on the ground—
like a man fallen asleep at a table,
his fist thrown forward. Church bells.

A Few Moments

The dwarf pine on marsh grounds holds its head up: a dark
    rag.
But what you see is nothing compared to the roots,
the widening, secretly groping, deathless or half-
deathless root system.

I you she he also put roots out.
Outside our common will.
Outside the City.

Rain drifts from the summer sky that's pale as milk.
It is as if my five senses were hooked up to some other creature
that moves with the same stubborn flow
as the runners in white circling the track as the night comes
    misting in.

The Name

I got sleepy while driving and pulled in under a tree at the side of the road. Rolled up in the backseat and went to sleep. How long? Hours. Darkness had come.

All of a sudden I was awake, and didn't know who I was. I'm fully conscious, but that doesn't help. Where am I? WHO am I? I am something that has just woken up in a backseat, throwing itself around in panic like a cat in a gunnysack. Who am I?

After a long while my life comes back to me. My name comes to me like an angel. Outside the castle walls there is a trumpet blast (as in the Leonora Overture) and the footsteps that will save me come quickly down the long staircase. It's me coming! It's me!

But it is impossible to forget the fifteen-second battle in the hell of nothingness, a few feet from a major highway where the cars slip past with their lights on.

Standing Up

In a split second of hard thought, I managed to catch her. I stopped, holding the hen in my hands. Strange, she didn't really feel living: rigid, dry, an old white plume-ridden lady's hat that shrieked out the truths of 1912. Thunder in the air. An odor rose from the fence-boards, as when you open a photo album that has got so old that no one can identify the people any longer.

I carried her back inside the chicken netting and let her go. All of a sudden she came back to life, she knew who she was, and ran off according to the rules. Hen-yards are thick with taboos. But the earth all around is full of affection and tenacity. A low stone wall half-overgrown with leaves. When dusk begins to fall the stones are faintly luminous with the hundred-year-old warmth from the hands that built it.

It's been a hard winter, but summer is here and the fields want us to walk upright. Every man unimpeded, but careful, as when you stand up in a small boat. I remember a day in Africa: on the banks of the Chari, there were many boats, an atmosphere positively friendly, the men almost blue-black in color with three parallel scars on each cheek (meaning the Sara tribe). I am welcomed on a boat—it's a canoe hollowed from a dark tree. The canoe is incredibly wobbly, even when you sit on your heels. A balancing act. If you have the heart on the left side you have to lean a bit to the right, nothing in the pockets, no big arm movements, please, all rhetoric has to be left behind. Precisely: rhetoric is impossible here. The canoe glides out over the water.

3

POEMS FROM:

Pathways (1973)
Truth Barriers (1978)

Elegy

I open the first door.
It is a large sunlit room.
A heavy car passes outside
and makes the china quiver.

I open door number two.
Friends! You drank some darkness
and became visible.

Door number three. A narrow hotel room.
View on an alley.
One lamppost shines on the asphalt.
Experience, its beautiful slag.

The Scattered Congregation

I.

We got ready and showed our home.
The visitor thought: you live well.
The slum must be inside you.

II.

Inside the church, pillars and vaulting
white as plaster, like the cast
around the broken arm of faith.

III.

Inside the church there's a begging bowl
that slowly lifts from the floor
and floats along the pews.

IV.

But the church bells have gone underground.
They're hanging in the sewage pipes.
Whenever we take a step, they ring.

V.

Nicodemus the sleepwalker is on his way
to the Address. Who's got the Address?
Don't know. But that's where we're going.

Snow-Melting Time, '66

Massive waters fall, water-roar, the old hypnosis.
Water has risen into the car-graveyard—it glitters
behind the masks.
I hold tight to the narrow bridge.
I am on a large iron bird sailing past death.

Further In

It's the main highway leading in,
the sun soon down.
Traffic backs up, creeps along,
it's a torpid glittering dragon.
I am a scale on that dragon.
The red sun all at once
blazes in my windshield,
pouring in,
and makes me transparent.
Some writing shows
up inside me—words
written with invisible ink
appearing when the paper
is held over a fire.
I know that I have to go far away,
straight through the city, out
the other side, then step out
and walk a long time in the woods.
Walk in the tracks of the badger.
Growing hard to see, nearly dark.
Stones lie about on the moss.
One of those stones is precious.
It can change everything.
It can make the darkness shine.
It's the light switch for the whole country.
Everything depends on it.
Look at it . . . touch it . . .

Late May

Apple and cherry trees in bloom help the town to float
in the soft smudgy May night, white life jackets, thoughts go
    far away.
Stubborn grass and weeds beat their wings.
The mailbox shines calmly; what is written cannot be taken
    back.

A mild cooling wind goes through your shirt, feeling for the
    heart.
Apple trees and cherry trees laugh silently at Solomon.
They blossom inside my tunnel. And I need them
not to forget but to remember.

December Evening, '72

Here I come the invisible man, perhaps in the employ
of some huge Memory that wants to live at this moment.
    And I drive by

the white church that's locked up. A saint made of wood is
    inside,
smiling helplessly, as if someone had taken his glasses.

He's alone. Everything else is now, now, now. Gravity
pulling us toward work in the dark and the bed at night. The
    war.

Seeing through the Ground

The white sun melts away in the smog.
The light drips, works its way down

to my underground eyes that are there
under the city, and they see the city

from beneath: streets, foundations of houses—
like aerial photos of a wartime city

though reverse: a mole photograph . . .
speechless rectangles in gloomy colors.

Things are decided there. No one can tell
the bones of the dead from those of the living.

The sunshine increases, floods into
cockpits and into peapods.

Guard Duty

I'm ordered out to a big hump of stones
as if I were an aristocratic corpse from the Iron Age.
The rest are still back in the tent sleeping,
stretched out like spokes in a wheel.

In the tent the stove is boss: it is a big snake
that swallows a ball of fire and hisses.
But it is silent out here in the spring night
among chill stones waiting for the dawn.

Out here in the cold I start to fly
like a shaman, straight to her body—
some places pale from her swimming suit.
The sun shone right on us. The moss was hot.

I brush along the side of warm moments,
but I can't stay there long.
I'm whistled back through space—
I crawl among the stones. Back to here and now.

Task: to be where I am.
Even when I'm in this solemn and absurd
role: I am still the place
where creation works on itself.

Dawn comes, the sparse tree trunks
take on color now, the frostbitten
forest flowers form a silent search party
after something that has disappeared in the dark.

But to be where I am . . . and to wait.
I am full of anxiety, obstinate, confused.
Things not yet happened are already here!
I feel that. They're just out there:

a murmuring mass outside the barrier.
They can only slip in one by one.
They want to slip in. Why? They do
one by one. I am the turnstile.

Along the Lines

(Far North)

I.

Sun glints from the frozen river.
This is the roof of the earthball.
Silence.

I sit on an overturned boat pulled up on shore,
and swallow the silence-potion.
I am slowly turning.

II.

A wheel stretches out endlessly, it is turning.
The hub is here, is nearly
motionless.

Some movement farther out: tracks in the snow,
words that begin to slide
past building fronts.

There's a hum of traffic from the highway
as well as the silent traffic
of the dead as they return.

Farther out: tragic masks bracing the wind,
the roar of acceleration. Still farther away
the rushing

where the last words of love evaporate—
raindrops that creep slowly
down steel wings . . .

Profile shouting—empty earphones
clashing against each other—
kamikaze!

III.

The frozen river gleams and is silent.
Shadows here are deep
and have no voice.

My steps were explosions in the field
which are now being painted by silence
that paints them over.

At Funchal

(Island of Madeira)

On the beach there's a seafood place, simple, a shack thrown up by survivors of the shipwreck. Many turn back at the door, but not the sea winds. A shadow stands deep inside his smoky hut frying two fish according to an old recipe from Atlantis, tiny garlic explosions, oil running over sliced tomatoes, every morsel says that the ocean wishes us well, a humming from the deep places.

She and I look into each other. It's like climbing the wild-flowered mountain slopes without feeling the least bit tired. We've sided with the animals, they welcome us, we don't age. But we have experienced so much together over the years, including those times when we weren't so good (as when we stood in line to give blood to the healthy giant—he said he wanted a transfusion), incidents which should have separated us if they hadn't united us, and incidents which we've totally forgotten—though they haven't forgotten us! They've turned to stones, dark and light, stones in a scattered mosaic. And now it happens: the pieces move toward each other, the mosaic appears and is whole. It waits for us. It glows down from the hotel-room wall, some figure violent and tender. Perhaps a face, we can't take it all in as we pull off our clothes.

After dusk we go out. The dark powerful paw of the cape lies thrown out into the sea. We walk in swirls of human beings, we are cuffed around kindly, among soft tyrannies, everyone chatters excitedly in the foreign tongue. "No man is an island." We gain strength from *them,* but also from ourselves. From what is inside that the other person can't see. That which can only meet itself. The innermost paradox, the underground garage flowers, the vent toward the good dark. A drink that bubbles in an empty glass. An amplifier that magnifies silence. A path that grows over after every step. A book that can only be read in the dark.

Calling Home

A telephone call flowed out into the night, and it gleamed here
and there in fields, and at the outskirts of cities.

Afterward I slept restlessly in the hotel bed.

I resembled the compass needle the orienteer runner carries as
he runs with heart pounding.

Citoyens

The night after the accident I dreamt of a pockmarked man
who walked along the alleys singing.
Danton!
Not the other one—Robespierre took no such walks.
He spent one hour each day
on his morning toilette, the rest he gave to the People.
In the heaven of pamphleteering, among the machines of
    virtue.
Danton
(or the man who wore his mask)
seemed to stand on stilts.
I saw his face from underneath:
like the pitted moon, half-lit, half in mourning.
I wanted to say something.
A weight in the chest: the lead weight
that makes the clocks go,
makes the hands go around: Year I, Year II . . .
A pungent odor as from sawdust in tiger cages.
And—as always in dreams—no sun.
But the alley walls
shone as they curved away
down toward the waiting room, the curved space,
the waiting room where we all . . .

For Mats and Laila

The International Date Line lies motionless between Samoa and Tonga, but the Midnight Line slips forward over the ocean, over the islands and the hutroofs. On the other side they are asleep now. Here in Värmland it is noon, a hot day in late spring . . . I've thrown away my luggage. A dip in the sky, how blue it is . . . All at once I notice the hills on the other side of the lake: their pine has been clear-cut. They resemble the shaved skull-sections of a patient about to have a brain operation. The shaved hills have been there all the time; I never noticed them until now. Blinders and a stiff neck . . . Everything keeps moving. Now the hillsides are full of lines and dark scratches, as on those old engravings where human beings move about tiny among the foothills and mountains that resemble anthills and the villages that are thousands of lines also. And each human ant carries his own line to the big engraving; it has no real center, but is alive everywhere. One other thing: the human shapes are tiny and yet each has its own face, the engraver has allowed them that, no, they are not ants at all. Most of them are simple people but they can write their names. Proteus by comparison is a modern individual and he expresses himself fluently in all styles, comes with a message "straight from the shoulder," or one in a flowery style, depending on which gang he belongs to just now. But he can't write his own name. He draws back from that terrified, as the wolf from the silver bullet. The gangs don't want that either, the many-headed corporation doesn't want it, nor the many-headed State . . . Everything keeps moving. In the house over there a man lived who got desperate one afternoon and shot a hole in the empty hammock that was floating over the lawn. And the Midnight Line is getting close, soon it will have completed half its course. (Now don't come and ask me if I want the clock turned back!) Soon fatigue will flow in through the hole burned by the sun . . . It has never happened to me that the diamond of a certain instant cut a permanent scar on my picture of the world. No, it was the wearing, the incessant wearing away that rubbed out the light and somewhat strange smile. But something is about to become visible again, the rubbing brings it *out* this time, it is starting to resemble a smile, but no one can tell what it will be worth. Not clear yet. Somebody keeps pulling on my arm each time I try to write.

After a Long Dry Spell

The summer is gray now strange evening.
Rain creeps down from the sky
and lands on the field silently
as if it intended to overpower a sleeper.

Circles swam on the fjord's surface
and that is the only surface there is right now—
the rest is height and depth
to rise and to sink.

Two pine trunks
shoot up and continue in long hollow signal-drums.
Cities and the sun gone off.
In the high grass there is thunder.

It's all right to telephone the island that is a mirage.
It's all right to hear the gray voice.
To thunder iron ore is honey.
It's all right to live by your own code.

A Place in the Woods

On the way there a couple of startled wings fluttered, and that was all. One goes there alone. It is a lofty building made entirely of open spaces, a building which sways all the time, but is never able to fall. The sun, changed into a thousand suns, drifts in through the open slivers. And an inverse law of gravity takes hold in the play of light: this house floats anchored in the sky, and what falls falls upward. It makes you turn around. In the woods it is all right to grieve. It's all right to see the old truths, which we usually keep packed away in the luggage. My roles down there in the deep places fly up, hang like dried skulls in an ancestor hut on a remote Melanesian island. A childlike light around the terrifying trophies. Woods are mild that way.

Street Crossing

Cold wind hits my eyes, and two or three suns
dance in the kaleidoscope of tears, as I cross
this street I know so well,
where the Greenland summer shines from snowpools.

The street's massive life swirls around me;
it remembers nothing and desires nothing.
Far under the traffic, deep in earth,
the unborn forest waits, still, for a thousand years.

It seems to me that the street can see me.
Its eyesight is so poor the sun itself
is a gray ball of yarn in black space.
But for a second I am lit. It sees me.

Below Freezing

We are at a party that doesn't love us. Finally the party lets the mask fall and shows what it is: a shunting station for freight cars. In the fog cold giants stand on their tracks. A scribble of chalk on the car doors.

One can't say it aloud, but there is a lot of repressed violence here. That is why the furnishings seem so heavy. And why it is so difficult to see the other thing present: a spot of sun that moves over the house walls and slips over the unaware forest of flickering faces, a biblical saying never set down: "Come unto me, for I am as full of contradictions as you."

I work the next morning in a different town. I drive there in a hum through the dawning hour that resembles a dark blue cylinder. Orion hangs over the frost. Children stand in a silent clump, waiting for the school bus, the children no one prays for. The light grows as gradually as our hair.

Start of a Late Autumn Novel

The boat has the smell of oil, and something whirrs all the time like an obsessive thought. The spotlight is turned on. We are approaching the pier. I'm the only one who is to get off here. "Would you like the gangplank?" No. I take a wobbly step right out into the night, and find myself standing on the pier, on the island. I feel soggy and unwieldy, a butterfly just crept from the cocoon, the plastic clothes-bags in my hands like misshapen wings. I turn and watch the boat go away with its lit windows, then grope my way up to the house I know so well that has been empty. All the houses at this landing are empty now . . . It is lovely to sleep here. I lie on my back, unsure if I'm asleep or awake. A few books I've just read sail by like schooners on the way to the Bermuda Triangle, where they will disappear without a trace. I hear a sound, reverberating, like a drum with poor memory. A thing that the wind thumps again and again against some other object the earth is holding tight. If the night is not just the absence of light, if night really *is* something, it has to be this sound. The sound of a slow heart heard through the stethoscope, it beats, falls silent a moment, comes back. As if its being went in a zigzag over the Border. Possibly someone is there, inside the wall, thumping, someone who belongs to the other world, but got left here anyway, he thumps, wants to go back. Too late. Wasn't on time down here, wasn't on time up there, didn't make it on board in time . . . The other world is also this one. The next morning I see a rustly branch with gold and brown leaves hanging on. A root body thrown upward. Stones with faces. The forest is full of monsters that I love left behind when the ship sailed.

From the Winter of 1947

Daytime at school: the somber swarming fortress.
In the dusk I went home under signboards.
Then the whispering without lips: "Wake up, sleepwalker!"
And all the things were pointing to the Room.

Fifth floor, facing the backyard.
The lamp burned in a terror circle every night.
I sat without eyelids in my bed, watching
the thoughts of the insane run on videotape.

As if this had to be . . .
As if my last childhood had to be smashed
into pieces so it could pass through the bars . . .
As if this had to be . . .

I read books of glass but see only the Other.
The stains that pushed their way through the wallpaper!
Those stains were the dead still alive
who wanted to have their portraits painted.

Until dawn, when the garbagemen arrived
and started banging cans five floors down.
Those peaceful bells of the alley
sent me each morning off to sleep . . .

The Clearing

In the middle of the forest there's an unexpected clearing that can only be found by those who have gotten lost.

The clearing is surrounded by a forest that is choking itself. Black trunks with the lichen's bristly beard. The jammed trees are dead all the way to the top, there a few solitary green branches touch the light. Underneath: shadows sitting on shadows, the marsh increasing.

But in the clearing the grass is curiously green and alive. Big stones lie around as if placed that way. They must have been foundation stones for a house, maybe I'm wrong. Who lived there? No one can help with that. The name sleeps somewhere in the archive no one opens (only archives remain young). The oral tradition is dead, and with it the memories. The gypsy tribe remembers, but those who can write forget. Write it down and forget it.

This little house hums with voices. It is the center of the world. But the people in it die or move away. The history ends. The place stands empty year after year. And the crofter's house becomes a sphinx. At the end everything has gone away except the foundation stones.

I've been here before somehow, but it's time to leave. I dive in among the briary underbrush. To get through it you have to take one step forward and two steps to the side, like a chess piece. Slowly it thins out and the light increases. My steps grow longer. A path wiggles its way toward me. I am back in the communications net.

On the humming high voltage pole a beetle sits in the sun. Under his gleaming shoulders his flight wings are lying, folded as ingeniously as a parachute packed by an expert.

Schubertiana

I.

Outside New York, a high place where with one glance you
    take in the houses where eight million human beings live.
The giant city over there is a long flimmery drift, a spiral galaxy
    seen from the side.
Inside the galaxy, coffee cups are being pushed across the desk,
    department-store windows beg, a whirl of shoes that leave
    no trace behind.
Fire escapes climbing up, elevator doors that silently close,
    behind triple-locked doors a steady swell of voices.
Slumped-over bodies doze in subway cars, catacombs in
    motion.
I know also—statistics to the side—that at this moment in
    some room down there Schubert is being played, and for
    that person the notes are more real than all the rest.

II.

The immense treeless plains of the human brain have gotten
    folded and refolded till they are the size of a fist.
The swallow in April returns to its last year's nest under the
    eaves in precisely the right barn in precisely the right
    township.
She flies from the Transvaal, passes the equator, flies for six
    weeks over two continents, navigates toward precisely this
    one disappearing dot in the landmass.
And the man who gathers up the signals from a whole lifetime
    into a few rather ordinary chords for five string musicians
the one who got a river to flow through the eye of a needle
is a plump young man from Vienna, his friends called him
    "The Mushroom," who slept with his glasses on
and every morning punctually stood at his high writing table.

When he did that the wonderful centipedes started to move on
the page.

III.

The five instruments play. I go home through warm woods
where the earth is springy under my feet,
curl up like someone still unborn, sleep, roll on so weightlessly
into the future, suddenly understand that plants are
thinking.

IV.

How much we have to take on trust every minute we live in
order not to drop through the earth!
Take on trust the snow masses clinging to rocksides over the
town.
Take on trust the unspoken promises, and the smile of
agreement, trust that the telegram does not concern us, and
that the sudden ax blow from inside is not coming.
Trust the axles we ride on down the thruway among the swarm
of steel bees magnified three hundred times.
But none of that stuff is really worth the trust we have.
The five string instruments say that we can take something else
on trust, and they walk with us a bit on the road.
As when the lightbulb goes out on the stair, and the hand
follows—trusting it—the blind banister rail that finds its
way in the dark.

V.

We crowd up onto the piano stool and play four-handed in F-
minor, two drivers for the same carriage, it looks a little
ridiculous.

It looks as if the hands are moving weights made of sound
    back and forth, as if we were moving lead weights
in an attempt to alter the big scale's frightening balance:
    happiness and suffering weigh exactly the same.
Annie said, "This music is so heroic," and she is right.
But those who glance enviously at men of action, people who
    despise themselves inside for not being murderers,
do not find themselves in this music.
And the people who buy and sell others, and who believe that
    everyone can be bought, don't find themselves here.
Not their music. The long melody line that remains itself
    among all its variations, sometimes shiny and gentle,
    sometimes rough and powerful, the snail's trace and steel
    wire.
The stubborn humming sound that this instant is with us
upward into
the depths.

4

From March '79

Being tired of people who come with words, but no speech,
I made my way to the snow-covered island.
The wild does not have words.
The pages free of handwriting stretched out on all sides!
I came upon the tracks of reindeer in the snow.
Speech but no words.

Fire Script

During the heavy months my life caught fire only when
     I made love with you.
The firefly too lights up and goes out, lights up and goes out
      —by quick glimpses we follow its route
among the olive trees in the darkness of night.

During the heavy months the soul sat
     indolent and crushed,
but the body took the nearest way to you.
      The night heavens gave off moos.
We stole milk from the cosmos and survived.

Black Postcards

I.

The calendar all booked up, the future unknown.
The cable silently hums some folk song
but lacks a country. Snow falls in the gray sea. Shadows
                    fight out on the dock.

II.

Halfway through your life, death turns up
and takes your pertinent measurements. We forget
the visit. Life goes on. But someone is sewing
                    the suit in the silence.

Romanesque Arches

Tourists have crowded into the half-dark of the enormous
    Romanesque church.
Vault opening behind vault and no perspective.
A few candle flames flickered.
An angel whose face I couldn't see embraced me
and his whisper went all through my body:
"Don't be ashamed to be a human being, be proud!
Inside you one vault after another opens endlessly.
You'll never be complete, and that's as it should be."
Tears blinded me
as we were herded out into the fiercely sunlit piazza,
together with Mr. and Mrs. Jones, Herr Tanaka and Signora
    Sabatini;
within each of them vault after vault opened endlessly.

The Forgotten Commander

We have lots of shadows. I was walking home
one September night when Y
after forty years climbed from his grave
and joined me.

At first he was entirely hollow, only a name,
but his thoughts could swim
faster than time could run
and caught up with me.

I set his eyes to my eyes
and saw the ocean in wartime.
The last ship he captained
rose beneath us.

The Atlantic convoy moved behind and ahead—
those destined to survive
and those who had received the Mark
(no one could see it).

Meanwhile sleepless nights relieved
each other but no one relieved him.
Life-jacket fat under his slicker.
He didn't make it home.

It was internal weeping that drained his blood
in a Cardiff hospital.
Able at last to lie down,
he turned into the horizon.

Farewell, eleven-knot ships! Good-bye 1940!
The history of the world ended here.
The bombers remained in air.
The heather went on blossoming.

A photo early in the century shows a beach.
We see six boys dressed up.
They have sailboats in their arms.
What serious faces!

Boats for some become life and death.
Even to write about the dead
is also a play that turns heavy
from the weight of what is to come.

Vermeer

It's not a sheltered world. The noisc bcgins over there, on the
    other side of the wall
where the alehouse is
with its laughter and quarrels, its rows of teeth, its tears, its
    chiming of clocks,
and the psychotic brother-in-law, the murderer, in whose
    presence everyone feels fear.

The huge explosion and the emergency crew arriving late,
boats showing off on the canals, money slipping down into
    pockets—the wrong man's—
ultimatum piled on ultimatum,
wide-mouthed red flowers whose sweat reminds us of
    approaching war.

And then straight through the wall—from there—straight into
    the airy studio
and the seconds that have got permission to live for centuries.
Paintings that choose the name: *The Music Lesson*
or *A Woman in Blue Reading a Letter*.
She is eight months pregnant, two hearts beating inside her.
The wall behind her holds a crinkly map of Terra Incognita.

Just breathe. An unidentifiable blue fabric has been tacked to
    the chairs.
Gold-headed tacks flew in with astronomical speed
and stopped smack there
as if they had always been stillness and nothing else.

The ears experience a buzz, perhaps it's depth or perhaps
    height.
It's the pressure from the other side of the wall,

the pressure that makes each fact float
and makes the brushstroke firm.

Passing through walls hurts human beings, they get sick from
    it,
but we have no choice.
It's all one world. Now to the walls.
The walls are a part of you.
One either knows that, or one doesn't; but it's the same for
    everyone
except for small children. There aren't any walls for them.

The airy sky has taken its place leaning against the wall.
It is like a prayer to what is empty.
And what is empty turns its face to us
and whispers:
"I am not empty, I am open."

The Cuckoo

A cuckoo sat cooing in a birch just north of the house. The sound was so powerful that I first thought it was an opera singer performing a cuckoo imitation. Surprised I saw a bird. Its tailfeathers moved up and down with every note, like a pump handle at a well. The bird hopped on both feet, then turned its body around and cried out to all four directions. Then it rose and flew muttering something over the house and flew a long way into the west. . . . The summer grows old and everything collapses into a single melancholy sigh. *Cuculus canoras* returns to the tropics. Its time in Sweden is over. It won't be long! As a matter of fact the cuckoo is a citizen of Zaire. I am not so much in love with travel any longer. But the journey visits me. In these days when I am pushed farther and farther into a corner, when the tree rings widen, when I need reading glasses. Many more things happen than we can carry. There is nothing to be astonished about. These thoughts carry me just as loyally as Susi and Chuma carried Livingston's mummified body all the way through Africa.

The Kingdom of Uncertainty

The department head leans forward and draws an X
and her earrings sway like the sword of Damocles.

As a spotted butterfly becomes invisible against the meadow
the demon slips in and merges with the opened newspaper.

A helmet with nothing inside has taken power.
The mother turtle escapes flying under the water.

Three Stanzas

I.

The knight and his lady
turned to stone but happy
on a flying mortuary lid
outside of time.

II.

Jesus held up a coin
with Tiberius in profile.
A profile without love—
power recycling.

III.

A wet sword
wipes out all memories.
On the field trumpets
and swordbelts rusting.

Two Cities

There is a stretch of water, a city on each side—
one of them utterly dark, where enemies live.
Lamps are burning in the other.
The well-lit shore hypnotizes the dark shore.

I swim out in a trance
on the glittering dark water.
A steady note of a tuba comes in.
It's a friend's voice: "Take up your grave and walk."

Island Life, 1860

I.

Down at the dock she was washing clothes one day,
and the deep-sea cold rose right up along her arms
and into her being.

Her frozen tears became spectacles.
The island lifted itself by its own grass
and the herring flag floated far down in the sea.

II.

Also the swarming hive of smallpox got to him
settled onto his face.
He lies in bed looking at the ceiling.

How hard it is to row up the stream of silence.
This moment's stain that flows out for eternity
this moment's wound that bleeds in for eternity.

April and Silence

Spring lies abandoned.
A ditch the color of dark violet
moves alongside me
giving no images back.

The only thing that shines
are some yellow flowers.

I am carried inside
my own shadow like a violin
in its black case.

The only thing I want to say
hovers just out of reach
like the family silver
at the pawnbroker's.

Grief Gondola #2

I.

Two old guys, father-in-law and son-in-law, Liszt and Wagner
    live on the Grand Canal
along with that nervous woman who is wife to King Midas—
I mean the one who turns everyone he touches into Wagner.
The green cold of the ocean presses upward through the
    palazzo floor.
Wagner has received the Mark, his famous Punchinello profile
    sags now
his face is a white flag.
The heavily loaded gondola carries their lives, two return
    tickets and a one-way.

II.

A palazzo window blows open; they make a face at the sudden
    draft.
Outside on the water the garbage gondola passes, oared by two
    one-armed thieves.
Liszt has composed a few chords so heavy one should send
    them
off to the Institute for Mineralogical Studies in Padua.
Meteorites!
Far too heavy to stay where they are, they start sinking and
    sinking down through the coming years until they reach
the year of the Brownshirts.
The heavily loaded gondola carried the hunched stones of the
    future.

III.

Pinholes toward 1990.

March 25: Disturbed about Lithuania.
I dreamt that I visited a large hospital.
No staff. Everyone was a patient.
In the same dream a newborn baby girl
who spoke in complete sentences.

IV.

The son-in-law, comparatively, is a modernist, Liszt is a moth-
    eaten grandsigneur.
It's a disguise.
The deep that tries and throws away various masks has chosen
    this particular mask for him—
the deep that loves to invade humanity without showing its
    own face.

V.

Old father Liszt is used to lugging his own bags through storm,
    snow, and heat
and when he arrives at death no one will meet him at the
    station.
A warm whiff of a highly cultured cognac carried him off in the
    middle of a commission.
He always has commissions.
Two thousand letters a year!
The schoolboy who has to write the misspelled word a
    hundred times before he can go home.
The heavily loaded gondola carries life, it is simple and black.

VI.

Back now to 1990.

I dreamt I drove a hundred miles for nothing.
Then everything got huge. Sparrows the size of hens
sang so loud that my ears closed up.

I dreamt that I had sketched piano keys out
on the kitchen table. I played on them, without a sound.
Neighbors came by to listen.

VII.

The clavier which has been silent through the entire *Parsifal*
     (of course it was listening) finally gets to talk.
Sighs . . . sospiri . . .
When Liszt plays tonight he holds down the sea-pedal so that
     the ocean's green force
rises through the floor and penetrates every stone of the
     building.
Good evening to you, beautiful deep!
The heavily loaded gondola carries life, it is simple and black.

VIII.

I dreamt that I was to start school but arrived late.
Everyone in the room wore white masks on their faces.
It was impossible to know which was the teacher.

(Note: *During late 1882 and early 1883, Liszt visited his daughter
     Cosima and her husband Richard Wagner in Venice. Wagner
     died several months later. Liszt's two piano pieces published
     under the title* Grief Gondola *were composed during that time.*)

TOMAS TRANSTRÖMER is the author of eleven books of poetry, most recently *For the Living and the Dead* and *Grief Gondola,* and a prose memoir, *Memories See Me.* His work has been translated into thirty languages, and has received the Petrarch Prize in Germany, the Bonnier Award for Poetry, and the Neustadt International Prize for Literature. Tranströmer and his wife lived in Västerås, Sweden, for many years, where he worked as a psychologist, and now live in Stockholm.

ROBERT BLY is a poet, essayist, cultural critic, and translator. He won the 1968 National Book Award in Poetry, and his two most recent collections are *Eating the Honey of Words: New & Selected Poems,* and *The Night Abraham Called to the Stars.* He lives in Minneapolis.

This book was designed by Wendy Holdman.
It is set in Concorde type by BookMobile Design and
Publishing Services and manufactured by Versa Press on
acid-free 30 percent postconsumer wastepaper.

ML   11-11